Walking with BASHO

POEMS, RAMBLES, AND RANTS

Jerry Lagadec

iUniverse LLC
Bloomington

WALKING WITH BASHO
POEMS, RAMBLES, AND RANTS

iUniverse books may be ordered through booksellers or by contacting:

iUniverse LLC
1663 Liberty Drive
Bloomington, IN 47403
www.iuniverse.com
1-800-Authors (1-800-288-4677)

Because of the dynamic nature of the Internet, any web addresses or links contained in this book may have changed since publication and may no longer be valid. The views expressed in this work are solely those of the author and do not necessarily reflect the views of the publisher, and the publisher hereby disclaims any responsibility for them.

Any people depicted in stock imagery provided by Thinkstock are models, and such images are being used for illustrative purposes only.
Certain stock imagery © Thinkstock.

ISBN: 978-1-4917-2623-5 (sc)
ISBN: 978-1-4917-2625-9 (e)

Library of Congress Control Number: 2014903141

Printed in the United States of America.

iUniverse rev. date: 02/22/2014

Contents

A Few Opening Remarks:

"A caterpillar,
this deep in fall—
still not a butterfly."

Matsuo Basho [1644]

Two Bashos inspired this book: Matsuo Basho, the master of the haiku—the poetry of brevity that captures complex emotions, images, and thoughts in three lines of 5-7-5 syllables, and Basho, our old Akita, a Japanese breed known for its strength, dignity, loyalty, and courage. They almost became extinct in the months after World War 2 when the Japanese, driven by desperation, used them for food and clothing. Thanks to Morie Sawataishi—who saved the last few—I've had Basho's company and friendship all these years.

I don't claim to have any profound answers or life—changing insights; I attempted to verbalize the feelings and thoughts that I've had when confronted with the enigmas of this existence. I tried to stay honest and weed out any note of falseness. I hope I accomplished that.

I've divided *"Walking with Basho"* into three categories:

Poems: Most of these were written after our daily walks. I dared to write haikus to accompany these; but like that "caterpillar", I'll let you judge if any of them managed to sprout any "wings".

Rambles: These are general, philosophical ruminations and observations that originated during our leisurely walks. We're both seventy and neither of us walks very fast.

Rants: Totally self-indulgent—We all need to let off some steam.

I dedicate this effort to my two walking partners: my wife Diane, whose support has been instrumental in getting me to stop doubting and procrastinating, and of course to our old Akita whose continued enthusiasm has inspired me to imitation.

I sometimes feel like a man stranded on an island, waving frantically to other island dwellers, hoping to muster enough courage to brave the shark infested waters.

I feel braver already.

If you're reading this book, thanks for "waving" back!

Two Old Dogs

Most mornings—weather permitting—Basho and I take a walk.

Named after that master of Haiku, he's a Japanese Akita, a breed known

for their samurai stoicism and silent dignity.

They practice an economy of bark; when they bark, you listen!

We're both seventy now-two old dogs out for a walk.

Our pace is measured but steady.

The assumptions of youth—when energy was boundless—have vanished.

Some mornings we decide to take a left into the mobile home park across the street.

We've made a few friends there: a couple of other elderly gentlemen who have lost their walking partners.

When we meet, Basho sits between us, waiting patiently as a congress of other old dogs speaks of loss and compensation.

Other mornings, we walk toward the lake around the corner and sit on the stone wall to watch the last shreds of mist drift slowly away like lethargic spirits, revealing the raggedy reeds on the shore line and the occasional snapping turtle moving in slow motion up a rock now being warmed by a blurry, red sun burning through the last bit of left over evening air.

Judging from the beads of sweat already trickling down my back and Basho's dripping tongue, it's going to be another scorcher!

We sit, touching, side to side, sharing the view—just two old dogs, imitating the stillness before the impatience of morning traffic and the angry growl of jet skis and motor boats begin.

"Silence—morning mist

Escaping off the water

No thought—this moment."

Abandoned Mary

She stands in a sanctuary of trees in her classic posture of outstretched arms and open palms.

Her church is closed, a bright red, garish "For Sale" sign shouts from the well manicured lawn still being attended to by an ancient, past parishioner who doesn't understand.

Above, a towering white spiral—topped with the symbol of man's cruelty, anguish and salvation—pierces the ocean of azure sky.

I want to steal her, take her home-a strange compulsion for a devout unbeliever-

and surround her with flowers and lush greenery.

In this time of brutality and impassioned voices screaming out their bloody dogmas,

her demeanor is a reminder that we must learn to transcend the darkness in our hearts.

When my friends would visit and the surprise would creep across their faces,

they know my doctrine of disbelief, I would say:

"We need all the help we can get."

> *"Two palms, empty hands*
> *Silence, sacred space, empty*
> *The bells still echo"*

On the Category of Pets
[A Rhyming Rant on Senior Moments]

There comes a time in your latter life

when you really should consider twice,

before deciding on which pet

would be the ideal one to get.

Yes, a dog's okay,

in almost every way,

perhaps even a ferret or a rabbit,

but not the long living, loquacious parrot.

For a parrot's years can equal ours

in months and days and human hours.

Not like a dog's that's 7 to 1.

There's really no comparison.

And parrots can get quite neurotic,

act bizarre and pathetically psychotic

when your demise precedes their own

and you bump off leaving them all alone.

So it's a sign of your extreme ineptitude

when in the throes of your decrepitude,

you get a parrot for a pet.

Cat-alyst
[A Ramble on Unexpected Inspiration]

This page is daring me to come up with something worth the marring of its pristine blankness.

I know I'm getting desperate when I resort to personification.

I am waiting for some insight, some imagery, anything.

Writing is a form of mental athleticism; you have to train, even when your muscles aren't willing.

I scribble thoughts and awkward phrases, anything to warm up those old creative synapses . . . but nada—nothing—no transmission—zero!

A mug of cooling coffee sits on the table, but even that didn't work this morning: no jolt of caffeinated inspiration came to unite the abstract and the concrete into some shred of revelation.

In frustration, I crumple my failures into tight, white, wrinkled balls, and toss them into the middle of the kitchen floor where they ricochet with a muffled bounce.

I'm about ready to give up, when Krishna races into the room and begins to knock them all about, chasing them with a joyous abandon.

I begin to write, catching the kinetic fire of this kitten's unmitigated joy.

You never know when you'll meet a master.

Waves

Basho and I sit by the lake, listening to the mantra of the waves chanting on the beach, the dull mutter of morning commuter traffic mumbling close behind us.

This morning I feel at peace; I haven't felt this relaxed in a long time.

In fact, I almost feel as present as Basho . . . but of course the minute you think about it . . . you're not.

We pay a price for our vaunted consciousness, especially when it turns in upon itself.

Maybe if we could just free ourselves from the learned habit of separating what moments deserve our full attention from those that don't, would we all be more like Basho and stop distracting ourselves with such silly speculations?

Now I am a thousand miles from here in time and place, floating above it all like some carnival balloon buffeted by every whimsical breeze . . .

when the synchrony of waves and breath brings me back . . . to here . . . now . . . with Basho . . .

A poem will have to wait.

"Two friends together

Whispering waves of mantras-

In the moment here."

Breakfast with God
[A Short Ramble against Passing the Buck]

Some religions forbid any representation of their deity.

Or they go the other way and have so many of them that you have to pause before praying, choosing the manifestation that best fits your needs.

They believe that the Source should not be limited, allowing more creative possibilities.

Since in the West we tend to have rather magisterial images in mind when we envision "God", it's understandable that we would have some difficulty with . . .

the disgruntled, grizzled Omnipotent One . . . sitting at his kitchen table . . . in his underwear . . . unshaven . . . yawning . . . shaking his head in frustration . . .

a cup of steaming coffee in one hand, a spiral of cigarette smoke wafting from the other, muttering to himself as he previews the "e-mails" of the day:

"Here we go again—endless prayers for mercy, pleas for understanding and kindness, more whining for compassion, love, justice, for the elimination of poverty and suffering!

Why the hell do they think I put them there for?"

Kinship
[A Ramble on Acceptance]

This is my wife's garden; my input is minimal, usually limited to tilling the groggy, winter soil and the occasional twisting of a rusty faucet during our occasional summer droughts.

But spring can be a wanton floozy, judging from the abundance of the invasive weeds and intrusive vegetation.

Diane had already begun and stopped, leaving one quadrant untouched.

I began to work, my back and legs aching from their unaccustomed posture.

It seems all forms of labor require a yoga specific to their demands.

"This used to be easier", I thought.

But then many things used to be easier.

And this reminder of my flagging flexibility and diminishing reserves brought to mind

a recent dinner conversation we had with friends.

Some might think the topic morbid, but it had to do with our wishes concerning the final disposition of our mortal remains.

Always the eternal romantic, I announced that I wanted my ashes spread in the garden and all around the only place that I had ever considered "home", a bit theatrical, I admit.

But it has always seemed to me that any frantic, futile attempt at some last minute subterfuge of stone and scripture is bizarre if not nonsensical.

I thought of all the times that I'd swept away those long abandoned, dusty cobwebs in our dry, dirt, cellar, left by spiders whose arachnid ancestors were weaving such tapestries long before the Pilgrims placed a foot upon that rock in Plymouth down the road . . .

I mused on all those winter nights, when I would stand in our back yard, shivering while staring at those crystalline pin points of winking silver, their sources long swallowed by the incomprehensible depths of that immensity of darkness.

I remember those times on late fall afternoons when I would pause and watch the giant, shriveled leaves and seed pods from our one remaining, majestic Catalpa mix with the wrinkled remains of the Elms and Maples; and I would see their deep green and smell those aromatic bouquets of hanging white clusters.

And now here I am with my aching back, my hands in the dirt, dwelling on all this . . .

when my fingers close about another bit of unwanted weeds . . .

and I am stunned by our future kinship.

July Morning

Lately-since I've discovered that my mortality is more than just another rumor from the provinces—I wake earlier.

Basho is still snoring, a light breeze softly lifting the white curtains above him while Krishna bound's up on our bed and wakes us with his swishing, Persian tail until one of us gets up to put out the food dishes that we store in a large white, plastic bucket.

It's an old house and many generations of mice have made their home here, long before we came along.

I don't mind that so much, but the little bastards can find their own mid-night snacks!

Afterwards, I sit on the porch with my coffee as a dull, pink sun begins to erase the last smudge of dawn.

Still in my pajamas, I'm shivering in the last breath of the night air, occasionally glancing at the slow climb of mercury on an old gage hanging outside by a solitary nail from the window frame.

Soon, I can feel the damp sponge of humidity squeezing down my back.

"It's gonna be a hot one!" . . . I say out loud to no one but myself.

Meanwhile, the morning shift is warming up like a bunch of sleepy musicians in the orchestra pit around us, taking over from the fading penny whistles of the night peepers from our pond below.

Then it all really begins: at first softly than joyously, rewarding

11

me for not rolling back to sleep the way I use to when I thought I had forever.

"The morning stirs, wakes

All the sounds of earth breathing

In celebration"

Shower of Acorns

There is telepathy between us now.

What is it: A subtle change in my posture, the rustle of the laces as I tie my sneakers?

Maybe it's the cats that give me away. They're usually discreet, but who knows what arrangements have been made between them?

But there he is-waiting—tail wagging like some crazy metronome to his rapid, excited heart beat.

He hates the gentle leader that I place around his muzzle; it's now as white as mine . . . when I forget to shave.

Akitas like to pull and he's no exception. Old as he is, he's still capable of dragging me wherever he wants, so this leader is a necessity.

Basho moves his head left and right to let me know that it's an agreed acquiescence but not servile capitulation.

He's not going to make it easy for me.

But this is the price and we pay it every morning.

We pause occasionally as he catalogues the thousand scents that we humans will never know.

Again we pause, as he marks his favorite trees and then scraps at the earth with his big paws, sending shards of dirt nowhere near their targets.

He's taught me a patience and respect for the needs and sensitivities of others.

I've wandered off into some sophomoric speculation on how to get a poem out of all of this . . .

when suddenly, a gust of wind sends down a shower of acorns.

"So lost in my mind,

Far away from this moment

Shower of acorns."

Gathering Morning Glory Seeds

I watch as your strong, nimble fingers break the dry seed pods into your palm and harvest their tiny black grains for next spring's incarnation.

These Morning Glories will return once more and entwine themselves around the weathered, graying staves of our garden fence.

I love that you do this; you could just buy a fresh new package instead of this meticulous and patient late September gathering.

These flowers have a history, a connection to this garden and your hands.

Basho sits in the shade of our towering pine, lost in Akita thoughts that we are not allowed to understand.

A lone wasp flies bye, seeking refuge from the cold to come as a gust of wind shakes the lawn umbrella above me and brings the acrid smell of burning leaves from the house next door.

And I'm here watching, hoping that someday the sight of Morning Glories will not flood me with a sudden agony too acute for me to bear.

"Cooling sun, black seeds

Your hands moving like dancers

Autumn afternoon."

Transplanting

When I was a kid, we would tear off the long, green seed pods from the huge Catalpa tree growing in our neighbor's yard. One of its boughs hung over our fence and these foot long pods were too tempting for young boys-drifting through summer vacation with too much time on their hands—to resist.

We called these long, skinny appendages "monkey cigars" and they really hurt when wielded as clubs, whips, rifles, arrows, spears, and other imaginary implements of war. They hurt even more when they dried out and turned leathery, their hardening, stiffening sheaths making them really lethal.

This afternoon, I am carefully transplanting a young, brazen Catalpa sapling that has had the audacity to take root in your garden.

My usual impulse would be to abruptly cut its roots, yank it violently from the ground, and toss it unceremoniously into the refuse pit behind the garden.

But I know how such wanton acts towards any living thing disturb you.

So—doing penance for my past insensitivities and transgressions—I amputate its roots with meticulous, surgical precision and transplant it to a place of full sunlight and ample space for its future roots and branches.

Then, wiping the dirt from my hands, I grow pensive and turn to you and say: *"I hope we're both here to see it grow!"*

And you smile, shrug your shoulders and say how lovely its aromatic, white blossoms will be for someone . . . someday.

"The dirt on my hands . . .

The knowing smile on your face . . .

Who will see it bloom?"

The Orange in the Trees

Today, driving down our country road, you pointed to the first, faint hints of orange in the trees.

Lately, I've become obsessed with such things:

Sunrises and sunsets,

Sudden storms and then the returning calm,

The evening hiss of tires on the still warm asphalt as I fall asleep,

The symphony of bird songs on those spring mornings when we start to wake,

All the risings and fallings,

The coolings and the heatings,

The strident caw of gulls and the break of waves on Duxbury beach,

The laughter of children in the playground, the burning leaves next door, the smell of simmering olive oil and garlic, the first sip of that strong, good morning coffee . . .

"Better late than never" is a saying that I've heard too often.

But now pain, like a returning warmth inching up a long frozen limb, informs my every moment. I wish that I had allowed this hurt to happen so much sooner.

But I didn't, because of another old cliché . . . you know . . . the one about *"not seeing the forest for the trees."*

"Orange in the trees

Green fading away each day

Bird song now and gone."

Unnamed Weeds

We took a walk this cold November morning.

It had not snowed yet and the ground lay hard and bare under a winter

world of faded browns and grays.

Basho stopped here and there, writing his own brand of poetry while you stooped to gather the spindly skeletons of . . . well . . . weeds . . . for we had no other names for them.

Once, in the moist heat of summer—among the more common verdancy of their less flamboyant neighbors—they had flaunted the reds, yellows, whites, and purples of the "Thistle", "Queen Anne's Lace", and "Celandine" that lined the road way in such chaotic abundance.

But now, they were indistinguishable, their proof of pedigree lost to the freeze of the Savage Great Reducer.

But you've always had a talent for finding beauty while others remained blind to its subtleties and deaf to its often silent music.

You saw it in our house, in spite of the callous disrespect of the former tenants who buried three hundred years of colonial history and husbandry beneath their bad taste and banality.

You found it in me.

And now you've found it in the poor dead, dried remains of these unnamed weeds whose reduction in grandeur renders them invisible to the less sensitive eye.

There is a sorrow in un-named things that often leaves them un-regarded.

You will bring your treasures home and arrange and display them in an old wine bottle, giving them one last resurrection and reprieve.

Once just unnamed weeds among the roadside trash and casual detritus,

now transformed into temporary art.

If only we could imitate them, in spite of the anonymity of our lost flowers.

"Sun, wind, light leaving.

Colors flee this winter world

Beauty masquerades."

The Forsythia Have Gone Crazy

I was startled by what I saw after an unusually warm, December night:

Our forsythia bushes were all blooming, brash yellow in the morning light.

Our forsythia bushes had gone crazy—they were blooming in December.

Now I know my memory's getting hazy—but I really can't remember

our forsythia bushes blooming in December?

I've read that the polar bears are drowning—their icebergs melting way up north.

The earth is turning drier, browning—while the verdict goes back and forth.

But our forsythia bushes were all blooming . . . in December?

Is this a warning like those poor gassed dead canaries in some deep, dark mine?

Or just a myth—like ghosts and fairies—fabrications of our mind?

Because . . . well . . . our forsythia bushes were all blooming . . . in December?

Now, I don't know much about history—know far less about biology,

but I do know that it's a mystery when something is that shouldn't be . . .

like our forsythia bushes all blooming . . . in December?

"Those yellow Blossoms

Against the browns of winter

Surprised and confused"

Two Tomatoes

You picked them green before the first frost and placed them on the window sill to ripen.

They will still be better than those tasteless, odorless ones that they sell all year at the supermarket down the street: such pale, anemic imitations of the ones warmed by the summer sun in our back yard garden.

Those you hold to your nose and are flooded by childhood memories

of running bare foot through the hot earth, ripping the reddest from its vine,

and biting into its velvet skin, reveling and rejoicing in the pink, sweet wine running down your cheeks.

Now the threats of winter surround me.

I mirror the fall in all its melancholy and metaphor.

Now I am at an age when everything is so much more than just itself.

All this from two tomatoes!

"Two tomatoes—green

Warming in late autumn sun . . .

I ripen with them."

Bowl of Onions

Half asleep, I stumbled into the kitchen to begin the morning ritual of tea and coffee: got to fill that kettle just enough but not too much or it will never boil.

Then I saw them: a modest mound of newly unearthed onions-

the last harvest from your late October garden.

I was caught by this un-intended still life.

For years, I've watched you bend in the first, warm promises of May,

planting your fetus bulbs and seeds into the newly upturned winter earth.

Now here they are, swaddled in a blue ceramic bowl,

their brown-yellow tendrils still reaching up,

prompted by some inner, reflex memory of sun.

Now onions . . . even onions—will never be the same for me again.

Faster than a master's stroke,

the ordinary is transformed into the intensity of private meaning.

"Autumn—your garden

Wind playing on chimes and leaves

Soon—harbinger flakes."

Backyard Pyramid

In our backyard, the foundation of a colonial barn has become our refuse pit:

Past Christmas trees—their dry, brown skeletons with clinging fragments of old tinsel sinking into the surrounding debris; bunches of rotting weeds and frost burned remains from our garden; shards of broken shingles from our old roof; the gathered Catalpa leaves with their long, hard dried seed pods; and all the other cast-off, vegetative bric-a-brac-

Anything deemed useless—winds up here.

But no paper or plastic: we recycle.

Today, as I tossed a few ragged, storm—wrenched branches into it, I stopped and marveled at the massive stones that once supported substantial walls and a heavy roof.

Quarried, hoisted, and transported here by human and real horse power, I stood in respectful silence, thinking about the old Yankees who erected such structures and cleared the surrounding fields so they could plant their gardens.

Their tumbled down walls of cleared stones are everywhere.

Even with all the proud constructs of our cleverness and the complexities of our technological contrivances, we will need to do a lot better to earn such future admiration.

Somewhere, thousands of miles from here, the blind, broken nosed Sphinx guards the pyramids as they cast their immense, ragged shadows across the Giza wasteland, their mangled symmetries testimony to the erosions of time, wind, and greed.

And now . . . here I am, impermanence, tossing impermanence into impermanence.

> *"Morning mist, red sun*
>
> *Both floating on the water.*
>
> *Announcing the dawn"*

Outside our Window

We put a Hummingbird feeder outside our kitchen window.

On summer mornings, I like to watch these fantastic creatures hovering with their blurred wings as they drink the syrup that I brew for them:

Four parts water and one part sugar—no red dye.

The color's for us and not for them.

The yellow plastic petals on our Job Lot feeder attract not only these delicate creatures, but also other stray contenders.

This morning there seems to be a battle going on between a hummingbird and a bee.

I stand transfixed, my cooling coffee forgotten in my hands.

What I at first took for a belligerent contest—is really something else:

First one . . . than the other . . . back and forth . . . repeated again and again.

Darwin-the misappropriated saint of the Age of Steam and Piston when rich men in black top hats held sway by claw and fang— knew of another law that somehow got conveniently misplaced.

Here it is . . . outside our window.

Someday, the dust of our greed and deadly belligerency may blow through the wasted, hollow places where once we failed to look outside our windows, and see what there was to see.

"The flutter of wings

Songs from every branch of trees

Ripples on the pond."

The Robin and the Sky

A deep silence fell over the Emperor's court as they viewed the vast canvas that covered the entire wall before them:

A single, delicate cherry blossom bow with a solitary robin, poised to take flight.

ChungTsu-fourth Emperor of the Tang Dynasty—finally spoke:

"Superb in execution and profound in its simplicity . . .

but why the vast expanse of empty canvas?

The master smiled and with a flourish of his hand replied:

"Robin and Sky . . . Sky and Robin . . . such is the Tao!"

The Emperor bowed.

"Robin, cherry bough . . .

Together in this moment . . .

Both to fly away."

Morning Prayer

The Doppler wash of early traffic . . .

The electric buzz of waking insects . . .

The hum of fans drawing in the last breath of night cooled air . . .

The insistent steam whistling on the stove . . .

The smell of coffee, browning toast . . .

Dust specks floating in a shaft of early morning light . . .

The soft rise and fall of Basho's white and brindle belly, his big paws bent as if in prayer . . .

The chirping of birds, the inquiry of owls, the scrambling of squirrels stealing seeds from the feeders outside the kitchen window . . .

Our cats racing from room to room, oblivious to everything except the ecstasy of movement . . .

All the precious, simple verses of my morning prayer.

> *"Again, the morning-.*
>
> *Verses at the start of day*
>
> *Prayer with no words."'*

After the Storm

The brutal hand of the storm came down and pummeled my carefully coifed lawn and grounds with a cruel ferocity, knocking down my meticulously architected wood pile, overturning the bird bath, and ripping away branches and leaves, leaving everything strewn about like the casualties from a bloody battle.

I viewed the after math of this conflict with a steely resolution: the forces of disharmony and discord would not win . . .

and then I got to work.

I carefully reconstructed my wood pile, attempting to improve its balance and distribution to avoid it falling victim to the next onslaught from our bellicose, New England weather.

I threw the broken branches and other debris into my wheelbarrow, dumping it all into the foundation hole from a defunct barn behind our house.

Leaf blower snarling, I begin the task of returning our yard to its original symmetry and grace, but the huge Catalpa leaves clung uncooperatively to the drenched earth like soggy paper.

I thought of the blood test I was scheduled to take in the morning.

Deep within the matrix of my cells, another storm is raging.

Some balances are not so easily re-established.

But then it is in the nature of all things to come together and then to fall apart in the eternal dance of the Tao.

Eventually, another storm will come and tear—with brutal disregard—the latest incarnations from their trees and I may not be here to fix or even witness it.

But for the moment, I am and I have work to do!

"Wind gone, ground covered

I work to regain order . . .

Futility smiles."

The Flamingo and the Buddha

There's a day-glow, pink plastic flamingo in our garden . . . next to a weathered,

concrete Buddha in his classic lotus posture of meditative repose.

I bought the Buddha many years ago at an up-scale garden shop for my wife's birthday—

the flamingo at a local Benny's where it waited—with its flock of kin-for discriminating connoisseurs of Chinese kitsch.

I wonder at the ingenuity of these artisans and entrepreneurs who

keep pumping out these endless variations of our cultural clichés.

The flamingo sports two black, rotating, clacking, propeller wings that

whirl with a joyous abandon to the tempo and whim of the wind, keeping the rapacious birds away.

Sometimes aesthetics and functionality fuse.

In contrast, the Buddha sits in transcendent silence, a faint wrinkle of a smile on his stony face.

The flamingo's frantic, mechanical exuberance well wear out long before the Buddha's equanimity is erased by the freeze and heat, the yin and yang of the spinning seasons.

On all of us, the patina and paint will eventually fade and flake, revealing the truth beneath.

"Smile on Buddha face

Winds moving the prayer flags

I watch in silence"

All around Me

In the back of our garden, a ragged, storm ripped, Tibetan flag snaps and ripples its Sanskrit prayers into a suffering world that needs them badly.

Next to it, a concrete, season stained, stone Buddha, its once glassy, factory glaze scoured into dullness by rain, sun, and frost, meditates on some inner, quantum world where zipping, sub-atomic particles contradict its outer, lotus still demeanor.

To my left a rusty bell sounds softly, its muffled voice annoying a swarm of hornets that circle angrily, their nest violated by this intrusion.

On my right—six, black, tubular chimes vibrate and vamp on their animated branch, their pure, clear tones almost palpable in the cool spring air.

Above—gusts of wind animate the newly uncurled, adolescent leaves into shivers of fluttering delight, lifting their undersides into spontaneous bursts of silver.

Behind me-in his pen—Basho does his laps in tight circles of intensity, wearing a deep groove in the gravel. Something's got him all worked up.

And here I sit, watching you work quietly with hoe and rake, my pad and pen idle in my lap, realizing that I will never write a poem quite as perfect as the one all around me.

But I have to try.

"Speechless by all this

Wind writing on bells and trees

While I scribble words"

."

October Rose

Today, on my way past the garden,

I paused to smell and touch the last, lingering rose of October.

In spite of the first onslaughts of autumn,

it still remained in redolent, ardent defiance of its eventual fate.

Around it, shriveled petals lay like the dirty, trampled confetti from a long gone, past parade.

Above, the yellow blisters on the leaves of the elms and maples spoke of the plague that was to come.

Before, youth afforded me amnesia of my irrevocable connection to such things . . . but now no longer.

Now, I sense the seasons turning, colors fading like some old photograph abandoned in a drawer.

I want to sink into the immediacy of all this.

I want to spend all my remaining coins of grief and joy

and to feel all things so deeply that I am left teetering on the edge of ecstasy and torment.

You have to try real hard to not become a poet.

.

"This last flower here,

Fading sun on wrinkled face-

Faint chill in the air."

Compost-ition

From the house to the compost bin and back, we've hung two sets of black, tubular chimes.

If there's no wind, a light brush of your hand will get them ringing, although it's difficult to imitate the winds, subtle, sudden improvisations.

-A piled high bucket of orange peels, coffee grounds, vegetable remains, melon rinds, cat hair and soggy teabags . . .

And a Pentatonic tune going down and a Mixolydian on return . . .

Yes, there's a time for taking out the garbage . . .

But you might as well make some music while you're at it . . .

or all you're left with is the garbage.

"Steel bucket—day's decay

Wild songs played by random wind.

Lotus in garbage"

The Last Leaf

Your eyes are blazing with the passionate intensity I've witnessed in other "true believers".

You know—your burning bush has told you so—"*There is no death! This life is just a trial, death a mere transition*",

and then the rewards and punishment dished out to the deserving and the damned.

Powered by an irrevocable certitude, you plead that if I could just shake off my doubts,

if I would just accept that there is a bright something . . . somewhere . . . and . . .

then you get a little vague . . . you start to stutter . . . cause . . . you know . . .

words can never really get it right . . . when you've been blinded by the light.

Meanwhile, above you, I watch a single, yellow leaf make its final, solitary journey to the ground.

All its kin had gone before.

It could cling no longer.

It falls with a spiraling grandeur in the random choreography of the wind.

I find its simple, silent elegance immeasurably more eloquent than any words.

This is the way I wish to exfoliate the withering of my flesh and the burden of my "self":

To let go and float away, mirroring this small thing's grace in not expecting more.

"Now time will vanish.

Fading with the dimming light.

Let go in this pulse."

Somewhere
[A Ramble for Letting Go]

When I die, I don't expect a movie score:

No crescendos of cascading violins . . .

No mournful Mozart Requiem . . .

No spiraling, solemn arpeggios . . .

Somewhere . . .

a truck will back fire . . .

A jack hammer will pound the tarmac . . .

A bum will wash a window with his filthy rag . . .

Another politician will impersonate sincerity . . .

A policeman will give a ticket . . .

A rich man will get richer . . .

While a poor man gets more of nothing . . .

A tired waitress will slip her shoes from her aching feet and count her tips while sipping on a scotch . . .

Pigeons will continue shitting on everything . . .

Sirens—like the one right now—will wake someone from their sleep.

And another set of eyes will turn to gaze out of this window at the dark matrix of the tangled limbs of trees that embrace this old, beloved house.

Somewhere, everywhere, it will all continue quite well without me . . .

And I thank the God that I don't believe in for what I had while I was here.

Supermarket Schadenfreude.
[A Ramble on Smugness]

*[**Schadenfreude**: that grateful feeling we often
get—although we'll never admit it-
when we hear of somebody's shitty luck
and we're so glad it wasn't ours.]*

This cloying, imperative of cheerfulness in this supermarket seems
to dredge from me the opposite response.

Perhaps it's the harsh, fluorescent glare, the endless permutations
of cereals,

the degradation of some of my favorite music into this syrupy ear wax.

Today, I'm at the nadir of my self-confidence, making a mental
list of all my real and imagined failures, all the defeats and
disappointments, all the humiliations of time and temperament,
all the residue of dreams gone rancid.

Like cornflakes, dreams also have a limited shelf life.

But then, as if my mood has elicited some reflex synchronicity of
compensation,

I see them . . . on the magazine rack before the check-out:

the untouched, un-flattered faces of the fallen famous expelled
from their former Hollywood Olympus,

their haggard expressions testimony to the cruel ravages of
whatever brought them to this tabloid low.

And now . . . here I am . . . in line . . . at the *"Stop and Shop"* . . . waiting for my turn.

This weary cashier—her name tag says she's *"Susan"*—is way too old to be standing behind this counter for so long, but her retirement check doesn't cover her expenses and her husband left without a warning so many years ago.

The man in line before me wears an oil stained, torn green shirt with the logo of a local garage and an emblazoned *"Joe"* over his heart where he keeps his cigarettes. His gnarled, grease encrusted hands testify to what he does for too many hours each day. He coughs violently into a dirty handkerchief as he places his bad but cheap food on the rolling rubber of the table. Those two packs a day will probably kill him but it's his *"one remaining vice"* he says and he use to have so many others that were far worse.

The frumpy, overweight young woman right behind me, wearing the food stained uniform of one of the many bad restaurants we have in town, attempts to calm a screaming and squirming infant while taking inventory of a rubber banded fist of coupons she cuts from the paper every Sunday night. Her name tag says to call her *"Dotty"*. She will grow old too soon and her dreams will fade like her once praised Prom Queen Beauty.

And here I am—an anonymous old man with bad eyes and too many doctors, attempting to compensate for my diminishing powers with these facile observations and imaginative extrapolations . . . and I am ashamed.

An Agnostic's Prayer
[A Short, Rhyming Ramble on Smugness]

Some speak of a recycling they've named reincarnation.

Others say it's all determined by predestination.

Many know who will rise to heaven and who will fall to hell.

I've heard some even count the virgins they will get, unlike those faithless infidels.

So many seem to be so very certain

of what awaits us all behind that final curtain.

Atheists say there's nothing—they're as certain as the rest.

But all this certitude seems preposterous if not presumptuous at best.

Because it's all the same old smugness, no matter how it's dressed,

So God, please save me from all these true believers,

from their madness and their rampant, raging fevers.

Protect me from their certitudes and concrete absolutes,

and most of all—from the crazies who claim to know the truth.

Autumn Minuet
[A Rhyming Ramble for the Long Forgotten]

The sun is melting into this lonely, cemetery ground.

The light retreats through the darkened trees—the wind's the only sound.

I see two stones both etched by sun and frost.

I push away the yellow leaves, the dry, dead grass and scrap away the moss.

Four years she waited while he went off to war.

He kissed her once-or was it twice—then vanished out the door.

They mailed him home in cedar shavings inside a crude pine box.

She went down to the depot and waited for the 10:15 to stop.

Following close behind the wagon, she thanked them and gave each one a coin.

Then began her twenty years of tears and longing—till she could finally join

her husband—here—together-as the sun begins to set-

two grey stony, shadows dancing in an Autumn Minuet.

Ten Thousand Cars
[A Ramble on Unintended Consequences]

We've all been there: racing down the interstate intent on our plans and then . . .

It's bumper to bumper, all stop and go, while the police wave and gesticulate in a ballet of emergency while strobes of blue and strident sirens say something bad has happened to somebody, somewhere way up there beyond the endless snake of steel and rubber winding around that curve on the far horizon.

Ten thousand cars now in stasis caused by some unknown,

incidental distraction in one mind, then magnified like

the slippage of tectonic plates, leading to a tsunami

that inundates the arrogance of our agendas.

That's all it takes to make the whole thing stop:

ten thousand possible glitches in our illusions of perfection, control, predictability and security.

Think about it!

The Wolves
[A Short Ramble for the Wisdom of Doubt]

You know, you'd feel so much better if you stopped running from those smirking wolves that lay in wait for you when the imponderable weight of this life seems too burdensome and unbearable and you long for the one trick pony of their promised certitude.

Only by devouring your doubts can they attain some momentary relief from their own hunger and self—gnawing.

I've watched their snouts rise when they sense vulnerability.

They know the "limp" of ambivalence that makes for easy prey.

Approach is everything: not too fast and not too soon.

First a smile and then a nod, and then a word and then some more . . .

all oiled with the unguent of their slippery guarantees.

But there is salvation in your insecurity and wisdom in your doubt . . .

if you don't sacrifice them to your fear.

So embrace it all, no matter how painful and distasteful, not some fantasy of bliss.

Get off your knees and stop your genuflection.

Then you'll sink into each moment with a weight you did not have when you mistook their howling for singing.

Apology
[A Ramble on the Unspeakable]

I remember a man, the same age I am now, sitting in a wheelchair in my mother's nursing home, a tray in front of him stacked with those plastic, pastel picnic cups . . .

just like the ones my mother would fill with iced lemonade and Kool-Aid and then bring out to me on those hot, summer afternoons, after I finished cutting the lawn with a push mower—boy powered—no motor.

He sat, intense in his dramatically diminished, yet determined concentration,

arranging those cups in infinite patterns and permutations.

Once—I was told—he had been a man of some intellectual prowess,

but a stroke had left him stranded in the cruel wreckage of his mind.

Placing and then replacing one cup over another, and then another, he worked feverishly, attempting to find his way back through some secret, alchemy hidden in the matrix of his designs.

His frustration was palpable.

I could feel my pulse pounding, my breath turning shallow and rapid.

There is a depth of empathy that can kill you, if you're not careful.

Our eyes met for a moment, and I stared down into my own terrors, frustrations and bewilderments.

Some memories are so powerful—they should never be weakened by words.

Some memories are so significant—anything but silence diminishes them.

Some memories are so disturbing-you should never reveal them.

I apologize!

Aisle Four
[A Ramble on the Lives of Others]

I am frozen in the florescent wash of this place.

I am in the cereal aisle where the shelves groan under an endless kaleidoscope of boxes picturing happy, grinning children; happy, grinning adults; sometimes happy grinning cartoon characters . . .

all fortified with the requisite vitamins and minerals to keep us all healthy . . . and happy.

It's what we need . . . to avoid possibly disturbing epiphanies of what's been done to bring this cornucopia of the world within our easy reach.

I flash on the wretched, mangled bodies of the collaterals of our insatiability that lie behind these charades of artfully contrived seductions.

I know . . . I know . . . it's a leap from cereals to corpses . . . admittedly a bit histrionic and disproportionate.

But I know that many others have paid a price for our programmed appetites, for our endless choices and demands . . .

It is more comfortable for me to not know then to know, so I must not follow the path that might lead me too near the edge.

Looking down, I might succumb to vertigo and forget what brought me here.

So I steer my cart along, in spite of that one, wobbling, errant wheel of conscience, my mind dulled by the lull of this carefully orchestrated atmosphere that pushes all my buttons of familiarity and annulment.

Besides, I have a coupon for a brand new something somewhere down aisle four.

Long-gone Julia
[A Ramble for Aunt Nettie]

Our "alzheimered" aunt sits in her bed, staring at a re-run of Chef Julia conjuring up—once again—one of her past gustatory spells, her pudgy forearms bulging with culinary contractions as she whips up some esoteric soufflé with a fancy French name that makes her lips pucker and contort like some deranged fish.

Long—gone Julia is riding her range once more.

Such reminders of the ephemera of existence disturb me, so I make a lame attempt at levity:

"She sure cook's great for a dead person!" Auntie likes that so much, she repeats my spontaneous quip, giggling like a schoolgirl at a naughty joke.

"She sure cook's great for a dead person."

She repeats it several times.

I am grateful for any momentary mitigation of the horror of watching her menu erased by the terrible hand of this disease, but I resist the next impulse to add:

"I wonder what's eating her now!"

I know that we are all part of this great gourmand universe that indiscriminately beats together the atom eggs of stardust, worms, and poets into infinite recipes of destruction and creation.

She repeats the line again with even more giggling gusto, and I see her vacating spirit flicker once more behind those dimming eyes.

The Law of Averages
[A Ramble on the Unexpected]

Deep in some dream, the jaws of nightmare suddenly opened beneath him . . .

swallowed once and he was gone.

It was reported on the Monday morning news:

"Sink hole opens up beneath man's bedroom."

His body was never found . . . in Florida, no less, the land of incessant sun and fun.

It sent a shiver of mixed emotions through me, a mélange of horror, fascination, relief,

with just a pinch of premonition, perhaps, recognition—

a scary suspicion that it's bizarre nature and suddenness could be closer to the truth than any of us are willing to admit.

How many, laying on a hard, cold sidewalk, surrounded by the faces of strangers, some concerned, some just curious, have— before being *"swallowed"*—thought:

"but I exercised, took my vitamins, practiced yoga, avoided saturated fats, drank responsibly, just had my checkup, took precautions, said 'no' to second helpings . . . ?

But thankfully, such thoughts pass quickly.

I am familiar with the law of averages and can relegate such bizarre occurrences to the realm of extreme rarity, trusting in those comforting statistics that dismiss any probability of my extinguishment in such a horrific, unexpected manner . . .

and yet . . . I bet—half awake—he started his day the same way:

with the aroma of brewing coffee mixing with the pungency of fresh, mowed grass and the perfume of early lilacs,

with the snarl of chain saws down the street, the barking of neighborhood dogs, the laughter of children waiting for their bus, a hundred birds singing up the dawn, the crash of garbage cans. *[Did I remember to put them out?]*

-all the familiar and comforting sounds and smells that help to create the daily rhythms of our lives . . . until some violation of the law of averages.

Basket of Dead Watches
[A Ramble on "Tickin"]

On my bureau: a basket of dead watches that I've been meaning to resurrect.

One belonged to Gene—my step-father—gold and silver, all fancy, flashy—who was born in the land of Virginia coal and joined the army at 15 to escape black lung . . .

and wound up living in California and driving a white Cadillac with Simone—my mother—a flashy, French woman with blazing red hair and a fiery tongue to match.

And then there's that old reliant Timex that *"takes a lickin', but keep on tickin"* . . . as John Cameron Swayze *[Goggle him]* use to say as he plunged it into a fish tank, or smashed it with a hammer, or dropped it from a ladder . . . each week inflicting one more act of stark abuse.

But even a Timex can get one too many *"lickins"*.

Then there's that stylish one-so thin-so unpretentiously elegant. I bought it when I had delusions that I could slip into my dotage while still maintaining some resilient panache.

But when time does the *"lickin"* . . . it's hard to keep on *"tickin'."*

My latest—not yet ready for the basket—is still *"tickin'"*. This one not only tells the time, but reports the current beats of my heart like some on—going metronome that monitors the rhythms of my life.

Like me . . . it's still *"tickin"*, in spite of all the *"lickins"* . . . at least for a while.

Omelettes
[A Mini—Ramble about Collateral Damage]

I don't understand those who judge their dogmas worth the mangled flesh of others.

I don't understand the bombings, bullets, knives, and fists of the holy, true believers.

I don't understand the easy speeches and phrases of acceptance . . . all the euphemisms for the necessity of murder.

I don't understand the abstractions that they use . . .

such as truth, freedom, justice, love . . . oh yes . . . especially love . . .

all employed in their permutations of annihilation.

But I do understand how easy it is to beat omelettes from the broken "eggs" of others.

The Incongruous
[A Ramble for Robert]

A mile down the street from our home, a wall is being built by two sun—burned men with weathered hands and mason hammers who hone each stone with practiced skill, chipping from the natural irregularities of the uncooperative rock, a harmony and balance that would have made old Euclid proud.

Hired by a millionaire, gentlemen farmer possessing the means to follow his own favorite phantom, they are making their way, foot by foot, creating a geometric boundary from the incongruent stones.

"Something there is" has already registered its objection to such presumption:

a small section of the wall has collapsed, sending random boulders back to their primal disarray, evidence of a devil in the frost that will not be easily subdued,

all testimony to a lack of love that a better poet once more eloquently expressed.

What is it about the perfectly flat, square, and sharply angled that intrigues us so?

I am left divided, deriving satisfaction from order, precision, and the propaganda of aesthetics . . . but also a bit disturbed.

I appreciate the potential dangers inherent in the vicissitudes of this scary life: the renegade cell, the faulty brakes, the tragedies caused by some momentary lapse of something . . .

But I also see the drifting, greasy ash of those deemed too "incongruous" to fit into the symmetry of someone else's Perfect Grand Design.

This Morning
[A Ramble on Random Suffering]

This morning, a starving old man in filthy rags is crawling from his cardboard shack in the slums of Mumbai. His aching hunger and the equally ravenous chiggers have not allowed him long to sleep. He scratches the swollen welts and wonders how he'll make it through another day.

This morning, orphaned children are already picking through the garbage in the dumps of Rio. They had to leave the city. The police were killing them for bounty, paid by merchants who said their begging scared away the tourists.

This morning, a homeless woman is rolling a shopping cart hung with black, plastic trash bags through the still dark streets of the Bronx, checking out all the dumpsters for bottles and half eaten fries from the local McDonald's.

This morning, a young man lies in his blood and filth, dying, flies settling on his face, hopeless and forgotten, one more pawn in the agendas of others. It was not always like this. Once—before the gangsters came to make them mine the metals for the cell phones that will be used in faraway cities—they had enough to eat and were lulled to sleep by the soft lowing of their cattle.

This morning, another infant born with AIDS will not make it till the noon. So soon, too short are the lives of so very many.

This morning, a mother is searching for her children through the rubble of the storm, clutching a rosary and mumbling frantic prayers. Around her the foul stench of corpses rotting beneath collapsed buildings fills the air like a malignant spirit intent on some new possession.

This morning, a man too haunted by the memories of war, his life too tattered to be mended by the words of those who mean well but do not really know, employs a bullet to stop the screaming in his mind.

This morning, a teenage prostitute, reapplies her makeup to cover the bruises on her face inflicted by her pissed off, brutal pimp for her poor night's profits

This morning, in some garbage strewn back alley, another needle claims its final nod.

This morning, I am sitting in my warm, safe kitchen, well fed and drinking coffee . . .

writing this poem.

Sour Old Men.
[A Ramble for the Disgruntled]

Driving down the road today, coming home from a morning of breakfast

and conversation with good friends in Plymouth,

I looked out the window and saw an old man sitting on his porch, a large mound of lobster traps rotting by the side of his house.

I thought: *"An old sailor too old and tired to pull those traps any longer."*

When I was a much younger man, I used to wonder about these old-timers wearing the sour discontent I saw on him that morning . . .

the same expression that threatens to settle on my face at times, as my jowls and chin wattle migrate south on the heels of all my other subterfuges of denial.

Given enough time, we all choose between two vessels to finish the final miles of this too short voyage:

One—false assuagements, desperate tactics to mitigate the obnoxious fate of being forever young aboard a creaking, leaking hulk.

This one won't make it out of the harbor.

The other—a begrudging acceptance that the life boats have dry rot, the charts don't match the water, the compass doesn't work, the captain is missing, and there will be no last minute rescue.

That one sinks right after sailing.

"So shove off Sonny . . . and leave me the hell alone!"

Remnants
[A Ramble for the Missing]

Christmas at our house is never quite over.

On the muggiest day of August you can run into a skating snowman hanging from a split head nail, wrapped in a cheery, colorful scarf of holiday red and green . . . do snowmen get cold?

Here-an angel spins wildly, caught in a hot draft from the window,

blowing his golden horn in festive enthusiasm, his cheeks puffed out like an ethereal Dizzy G.

There—another rosy cheeked Santa on ice skates, arms spilling multi-colored packages . . .

Dusty, silver snowflakes hang everywhere.

Baskets of old cards from Christmases past sit on our round spool table.

On the piano, a melting, ornate Christmas candle sent to us by my parents when we first got married. They are gone and we are much older now ourselves.

It's a violation of the Hall Mark Code of Cheer to dwell too long on the missing: parents, wives husbands, brothers, sisters, friends, even pets, and sometimes-sadly-children.

But it's true, none the less.

We can't escape the cruel ferocity of time that inspires our need to reproduce those rituals made sacred by our memories of love.

The Prince of "Pieces"
[A Short Rant on Cognitive Dissonance]

I know a good, God—fearing Christian.

He's always "packing"; he's never without his *"piece"*—a "38" were his exact words.

Yep . . . armed and ready . . . always . . . he's *"never without it"*, he stated proudly.

I asked him *"why "*-as delicately as possible—didn't want to piss him off.

His answer was a bit rambling and obtuse; I lost the thread.

It was something about an angry Jesus losing it and going ballistic on those who defiled the sanctity of the temple.

That example gets used a lot, I've noticed.

I believe the implication was that Jesus was no pussy, no "hippie", no way; he was a man's messiah and knew how to administer some of that *"tough love"*.

I flashed on a scene in an Alternate Universe:

Jesus, after terminating with extreme prejudice all those cretins in the synagogue, is reloading his extended capacity clip in the garden of Gethsemane—thank God for the NRA . . . ready to rock n' roll!

His disciples—agitated; they've heard stories . . . whispers . . . and Judas is missing.

Enter Pilate's belligerent Roman Centurions, primed for trouble.

"Then it's—*bang!* . . . *bang!* . . . *bang!* . . . etc . . . etc . . . etc.

End of story!

Everybody go home!

Work out your own salvation.

There goes one major holy holiday.

The Bunny wins!

Worldly Things
[A Rant for "the here and now"]

Taking a break from our early morning walk, Basho and I sit by the lake, looking out over the curling peaks of waves whipped up by a stronger than usual wind that wrenches the last leaves from the trees and rips away at the lawn umbrellas still up on the shoreline.

The air is an October stew of cooling water, blowing leaves, acidity pine and dead weeds . . . all simmering in a bitter piquancy of exhaust.

On our way home, we pause at the mailbox to collect the daily assortment of bills and come-ons.

This morning there's a slick, glossy promo from a local church.

I read a bit: it seems to have a lot to do with spending all eternity singing fawning praises to some egomaniacal deity.

There is a warning written in bold, dark type:

"Don't place your trust in worldly things; prepare yourself for eternity."

Exactly what they're referring to with **"eternity"** is left quite vague, creating a vacuum which demands a fleshing out with whatever images I can concoct from the current pabulum and mish mash that's passed off as "religion".

If you've ever chanced upon one of those Gideon Bibles in drawers of mid-western motels, you'll know what I mean:

Jesus sitting on a rock surrounded by adoring little children dressed in the appropriate costumes of politically correct racial and cultural diversity with white mansions gleaming in the background, all surrounded by well manicured lawns serviced by wet-back angels earning their celestial green cards. It's not hard to imagine the Savior tossing around a Frisbee while the burgers are cooking on the grill, the entire scene the very apotheosis of a suburban cook-out.

I can't help but to extrapolate on the implied consequences of my recalcitrance to leave my "***worldly things***" behind:

If I don't acquiesce to this vision of ethereal ass kissing, I will be just one more poor sucker locked out at those pearly portals—decorated with chubby, frolicking cherubs—listening to the strains of heavenly cocktail music, the tinkling of crystal glasses and the laughter of the chosen, all while waiter angels buzz about like manic hummingbirds, serving canapés of cloud pate and chilled champagne distilled from distant star shine.

Sounds like hell to me!

You're going to have to give me something more to go on before I forego the pleasures of **"worldly things."**

You see, I like this vivid, pungent place, even when it hurts like hell and scares the living shit out of me!

I like experiencing, savoring the smallest, simplest things in the "here and now".

I like the fundamental "goodness" I find in even the most imperfect people that I meet.

I trust that . . . in them . . . in me.

I like the mystery that hides in the mundane, waiting to be discovered, if you stop, slow down, and really look.

I didn't come here to obey, to bow my knees or head to some magical construct born of the needs and fears of others.

So you see, I haven't got a chance to make it up to those lofty heights.

I'm pretty certain that this life, this one here, right now . . . is all I can really trust.

You either figure that one out for yourself . . . or you don't.

You won't find me stuffing a promo in your mail box.

*Thank God for **worldly things!!***

Hunky Jesus
[A Rant for the Real]

Jesus is smiling at me from the calendar display at Staples.

I have to tell you, this is one hunky Jesus, not that retro, dark—skinned version with his hooked nose and dirt—encrusted robe.

No way—not this Hunky Jesus!

Oh . . . and that beaming, Rorschach smile that promises salvation . . . in any shape and size, in any form . . . or not.

He should have crossed tennis rackets or maybe one of those little green alligators embroidered on his impeccably tailored, spotless white robe.

He's definite proof that the Semitic races floated up North on their rickety rafts of reeds and vines.

Bet he even smells nice, not like that other one who stank with sweat and grime from wandering the roads of Jerusalem and Palestine, preaching the primacy of love.

This Jesus is an ad man's dream:

Handsome, self-assured, golden tresses coiffed to perfection,

his skin—a perfect life guard gold.

And those eyes—oh those eyes—deep enough to make a nun think the unthinkable.

You get the picture.

Next to him, a smiling Marilyn leans provocatively on an upturned umbrella, ready to receive her Savior in the same posture that once launched thousands of greasy pin-ups on garage walls everywhere.

Justin Bieber's there—ready to set adolescent hormones raging.

And Dr. Seuss, the Beatles, those Sports Illustrated Bimbos, Peanuts, and dozens of unbearably cute kittens and puppies . . . all there . . .

all the images and characters that keep the "wheels" in our heads spinning.

Snoopy and the Baby Jesus
[A Zen Rant]

While walking out of Benny's today, I paused before a nativity scene: a crèche with the iconic figures of Mary, Joseph, the Wise men, the customary barnyard animals and—of course—

the Baby Jesus, swaddled in his crib of Chinese plastic.

I've seen these garish figures of the Holy Family before, but this time my attention was drawn to an incongruous addition: Snoopy, Schultz's cartoon beagle creation.

He seemed ready to launch into that famous, frenetic dance he does when overwhelmed with joy and words are not enough.

He seemed comfortable, to fit right in.

But did I detect a faint hint of a grin on Snoopy's face?

The same hint that I'd noticed on the stone Buddha in our garden?

You know—that subtle wrinkle of a smile-the often irritating one you see on people who seem to . . . well . . . have "it" . . . get "it" . . .

"Irritating" because sometimes . . . they do!

A few attempt to explain "it"; most don't bother—they know that "it" will get distorted in translation and transmission.

We all want "it", whether we know it or not; and when we do get "it"—we realize we had "it" all along . . .

because . . .

There's nothing to get.

There's nothing to do . . .

In fact—there's really no one to get "it" or do "it" . . . and that's how you get "it".

Snoopy's got "it"; Buddha's got "it"; Jesus' got "it";

and we all have "it" too!

Dead Men Singing
[A Seasonal Rant for "Hope"]

Is it just me . . . or is there something just a little bit off-putting with all those long—gone dead men singing Christmas carols in the local mall?

I know, I know, you're probably thinking:

What's the difference between them and all the other dead guys singing on the golden oldies station?

Well, context is everything.

Christmas is the ultimate happy season of amnesia when we—for a time—forget the dread of our mortality, and replace those dark thoughts of dying . . . with buying.

So let Burl tell you to: *"Have a Holly, jolly Christmas . . ."*

Let Gene tell you—once more-about old Rudolph *"with his nose so bright . . ."*

Bing will croon about the special night when *"all is bright"* . . . *all is calm"*

while Nat sings of *"chestnuts roasting on an open fire . . ."*

as Dean slurs *"The Little Drummer Boy"* . . . after three bourbons and a Las Vegas hooker.

Ok . . . I know! I'm a cynical old curmudgeon.

You may be right; what the hell do I or any of us know for sure?

When you get right down to it, we aren't given much to go on.

So sing it out, guys: all the holly jolly, flying reindeers, and keep those chestnuts roasting!

Yep, keep on singing because this life is tough enough and there's no reason to make it harder.

Beat that drum son cause *"tis the season"* . . .

Maybe, just maybe, we <u>will</u> all rise up on that first morning after the last ding dong of time and run to see what Santa left. That's all I want for Christmas!

Satchmo's Sutra
[A Ramble on "Shu-bop—Shu-bop"]

Gautama looked out upon the vast throng

that had been gathering since dawn.

Word had traveled faster than the ebbing monsoon rains

that had drowned the world around them.

They had heard about his awakening and they were there

to hear the sutra that would set them free.

Above, the leaves of the Bodhi tree, saturated with his satori,

dripped down its drops upon the head of an ancient monk

who had limped painfully on his bamboo canes from so very far
to hear Siddhartha speak.

Leaning forward, the Buddha beckoned toward him to come
closer.

The monk's face, deeply lined with the scars of his many years,
shown with a transcendent light as he discovered that the pain
and stiffness in his aching joints were gone.

He cast his canes aside and approached the Enlightened One.

He leaned forward and he began to laugh as the Master hummed
into his ear, softly snapping his fingers.

The infectious melody seized the devotees and soon they were all on their feet, singing, dancing . . .

until exhausted, they fell into a profound sleep.

When they awoke, they were alone and began to argue and to doubt their former state of bliss.

It is a weakness inherent in most men that leads them to mistrust their capacity for joy.

And like all great truths, this one was lost in flawed attempts at translation; most men are faulty transmitters of such things and the Sutra's power weakened until it became the subject of the arrogant squabbles of self—important men.

Pilgrims, seers and fools alike would argue its mysterious wording.

Monks in orange and ochre robes would clap their hands and stamp their feet in hot debate.

Kings would hold court with the most august of assemblies to ponder its perplexing ambiguities.

Wars would be waged, peace would return, empires rise and crumble, and it would still remain a mystery . . .

Until one man put aside his golden horn, snapped his fingers and sang:

> *"It don't mean a thing . . . if it ain't got that swing . . .*
>
> *Shu-bop-Shu bop!"*

Mercy
[A Rhyming Ramble for another Chance]

We need more possibilities about another "something" . . . after this:

We're either singing with the angels or being stabbed with sharpened sticks.

I rather like the one that says you get all the chances that you need—until you get it right.

It's as good as any other that might help us through the night.

Besides, when all the talking's done

there's very little that we know for certain.

We play our parts and recite our lines before the final curtain.

After that, well any guess is just as good as mine.

So why not just relax and keep all possibilities in mind

and admit that we're making all this up as we go along.

Some theories might be half way right—while others half way wrong.

So you can believe in this . . . or maybe even that.

We can argue now and probably for ever about what's fiction or what's fact.

But I'd rather hope for one more chance if I've really screwed things up

cause when it comes to mercy, we never give or get enough.

Hardware Horny
[A Rant on the Gratuitously Erotic]

The Buddhists advise against exploiting our passions.

Unlike others, they don't threaten: no eternal, burning damnation with requisite brimstone and agony-no leering devil minions, gleefully prodding the fallen with their pointy, flaming pitchforks . . .

but they do warn that if we continually promote our lusts, we will keep coming back in endless incarnations until we free ourselves from these repetitive habituations.

Now—I'm not saying I believe this without question, but if there is the slightest chance that there's something to it, I'm going to pay more attention because, frankly,

I am a bit ambivalent about this life, whether the pleasures are worth the pain, the delight, the subsequent decay.

I walked into the local hardware store today, looking for some screws.

And there she was: a tool belt around her tiny waist—and not much else—posing in a cardboard posture of tantalizing, erotic enticement, her delicate, manicured fingers fondling the latest phallic permutation of a large electric drill.

It wasn't the kind of screwing that I had in mind!

Auntie Pain
[A Rant for the Youthfully Deluded]

Get use to it kids!

There will come a time when pain will no longer be just a momentary inconvenience; it will be like that irritating Aunt that visits you in the hospital-as if your busted leg weren't enough.

"Hi . . . . I brought you some magazines and candy. Try the bonbons. They're yummy. Are they treating you right here? Is there anything you need"? Whew . . . is it always this hot in here? You know I had my gall bladder taken out here by Dr . . . Dr . . . oh what was his name? A short chubby Jewish guy with big glasses and . . . you sure you don't want one of these? Sooo good! Oh anyway, did you hear about your uncle Phil? Well I always suspected that she was no good. The way that woman use to dress and she couldn't cook worth a damn. I had some pot roast there once and had gas all night! Oh, I tried to warn him but would he listen? Not him and then she ran off with . . . .

and *"blah, blah, blah!"*

In fact, she talks the staff into letting her sleep in the bed next to you, but she never sleeps: She just talks and talks and talks.

So next time you start crabbing about a world that does not give you what you think you deserve,

remember, that Auntie Pain is on her way.

She's out there, buying a ticket, and stopping to get you a box of candy that she'll eat and magazines you won't read, and boy, does she have some juicy gossip for you!

Busted Umbrella
[A Rant on Awkward Things]

What do you do with a busted umbrella?

You can't open or close it—it's busted.

It's Mary Poppins' nightmare.

You can usually figure out lots of stuff to do with other things that no longer fit their original job description:

Cans—great for nails

Bottles—nice for flowers

Cardboard Boxes—ask my cats.

Bits of Clothesline—tie things up

Pieces of Plastic—in case it rains

Crap in your Attic—big yard sales.

Clothes that you don't wear—perfect for scarecrows.

And if you don't know what to do with something, but you just can't seem to throw it out, there's always some book written by some hoarder somewhere who can suggest clever reincarnations.

But a busted umbrella?

It's the end of the line!

You can't bag it; it'll tear the hell out of those flimsy trash bags.

So the trash men won't take it; even they have standards.

You can't bring it to the dump, at least not by itself.

You'll raise suspicions:

Maybe he bludgeoned his wife, his obnoxious neighbor . . . or maybe some barking dog?

No, you're stuck—you have no clue of what to do with it.

It just loiters about, leaning in the corner like some sneering, smartass teenager with his baseball hat on backwards and his clown pants hanging down to the crack of his ass—daring you to do something.

Lobsters from Outer Space
[A Lengthy Rant on the Therapy of Kitsch]

I confess to a guilty pleasure: low budget, classic Science Fiction movies, ones you might see on *"Creature Feature"* every Saturday at mid—night.

I admit to "guilt" since most educated people—the ones who've read the *"Great Books"*-

would summarily dismiss me as a moron for wasting my mind and time on tributes-like this—to truly bad taste . . . or . . . for you English Majors, this *"Homage to Kitsch."*

But then, I'm not claiming they're "Art";

I'm talking about one of the least known forms of personal therapy.

I confess: I am . . . shudder . . . one of those—*"English Majors."*

I didn't plan on this anymore than I planned on being a member of AARP . . . but I am . . . in both cases.

Anyway, how I settled on a career path that's usually chosen by those who have no idea what they really want to be or do in this life was a result of my dorky answer to the authorities when they asked me to declare my "major":

"I dunno . . . I like to read?" [I am a dork!]

I didn't tell them that I especially enjoyed trashy science fiction and horror paperbacks: the mildewed ones you might find in abandoned cabins next to empty bottles of cheap booze and bad porno.

But it didn't matter; the label came down like an ax on a chicken : *"English Major"*.

I'm only telling you this to explain how this fateful decision has contributed greatly to my neurosis: my sense of being a colossal fraud, a poseur, a pseudo-intellectual who would rather read Stephen King than be subjected to the preachy, cloying sermonizing in *The Scarlet Letter*.

I admit it: I need therapy! Ergo—this rant . . .

But before you dismiss me as a total Philistine,

allow me to elaborate on a few positive, unintended consequences— benefits if you will—of these grotesque Sci-Fi deformities that plod along like dying draft horses, hauling loads of putrid scripts, low budget, not so special effects, inane story lines, a thespian level better suited for fifth grade re-enactments of *"The First Thanksgiving"*, and totally incompetent direction, if any.

- First of all—it really is" *the singer, not the song."* Imagine having to deliver: *"I may be able to fix the hyper—molecular disintegrator and save the earth from the Gorgons . . ."* and not double over with nausea, if not hysterical laughter.
- And what about the ability to scream convincingly when being confronted by a "Gorgon", an alien monster— curiously resembling a Maine lobster—that possesses not even the slightest modicum of verisimilitude? [*English Major*] I mean, a little putty here and there to aid the suspension of disbelief would have been in order . . . but alas "credence" was boiled and then gutted like . . . well . . . a lobster at the *Seafood Shack*.
- *Universal truth*: everybody has to start somewhere . . . even

if you don't get very far. Once in a while you'll discover—in the final credits—the name of some now famous star who began his/her career in one of these turkeys and continued hanging in, delivering lines [written by a recently arrived immigrant from the Ukraine with ADD . . . and an uncle who financed the film.] all while climbing down a poorly disguised step ladder from a spray-painted, cardboard flying saucer to . . . yes . . . fight the lobsters . . . I mean the *"Gorgons"*.

- The music: some maestros—now directing world famous Philharmonics—began their careers lending their considerable talents to complementing the stumbling, awkward attack of the *"Gorgons"* . . . soon to be dispatched by the *"hyper—molecular disintegrator"* that one of the *"Teenagers from Outer Space"* manages to fix with a soldering iron and toaster parts.

- *The therapeutic value*-the most important service these celluloid mistakes can render. Don't we all sometimes find ourselves depressed when we compare the ambitious goals we once set with those we have actually achieved? Don't we all—at times—get down on ourselves for our real or imagined shortcomings? But I challenge you to find anything in your history of screw-ups and stupidities to match the abyssal level of inanity found in . . . oh . . . Ed Wood's *"Plan 9 from Outer Space"*.

- *Schaudenfreude*: a German expression that translates as the pleasant glow you experience after viewing one of the films listed and thinking: *"Man, at least I didn't make this piece of crap!"* It's that warm, smug sense of relief you get when passing the dreadful wreck on the highway or the self congratulatory feeling when witnessing that obnoxious drunk attempting to play the drums at your sister's wedding.

- *Compassion:* They had dreams; you had dreams . . . in a universe that doesn't give two Gorgon turds about them—work with this!

Watch a couple of these and call me in the morning; you'll feel so much better, realizing that most of us have to do the best we can with what we're given. You'll notice a certain "space" theme that's less "cosmic" and more 'cerebral", better describing the crippling, synaptic distance between neurons in the minds of those responsible for these lobsters . . . I mean *"Gorgons"*.

1. *Plan 9 from Outer Space*
2. *Evil Brain from Outer Space*
3. *Killers from Space*
4. *Assignment Outer Space*
5. *Attack from Space*
6. *Warning from Space*
7. *Teenagers from Outer space*

They're a lot more fun than electro-shock.

Fine Cuisine
[A Short Rant on the Death of Irony]

I'm pumping gas and I notice this guy in front of me with one of those chrome sided trucks that go around to construction sites selling Saran wrapped sandwiches, bad coffee, Twinkies, Eskimo Pies, and a whole lot of other trans—fat crap snacks to guys in hard hats with muscular pick-ups loaded with patriotic stickers and decals of smiling punks pissing on the logos of the other guy's brand of truck . . .

when I see this inscription boldly emblazoned on the back and sides of his truck:

"Wally's Snacks and Fine Cuisine*"*

I watch Wally roll from the cab, his gelatinous jowls shaking in a lardy synchrony with his ponderous belly, chomping on a bleeding jelly doughnut,

and I don't know what to think!

The Random Roach
[A Rhyming Rant on the Truly Stupid]

Now it's a fact—almost too obvious to be mentioned

that our demise can happen in an assortment of dimensions:

An errant spark and it's all over

and unruly cell—you're pushing clover.

You fall asleep—you don't wake up.

You zig—don't zag—you're out of luck.

And then how about all those wars, diseases and stupid mishaps,

a thousand household slips and fatal, unexpected accidents.

But let me tell you about a guy who died after gorging on a dish of roaches!

I read about it in a magazine so please—save your accusations and reproaches.

He croaked after scoffing down a plate of those creepy, crawly, many legged insects;

the ones who multiply in dirt and filth and indiscriminating incest!

We could dismiss this all as just a quirky, idiosyncratic, bizarre perversion.

Maybe he was bored and needed some new sort of diversion.

But no—there were others; this was a sponsored, community event—

in fact, a contest—it was planned and absolutely meant.

Now, I must admit I find it rather strange

that so many were so equally deranged . . .

but the really disturbing thing was . . .

well . . .

my curiosity's was raised because . . .

No one else who ate this repulsive dim-sum died-

in fact, they thrived, survived . . .

except for him!

Now, the experts offered their official explanation

to discourage any unnecessary, foolish speculation.

"His roaches—only his—were infected with a virulent, random, rare bacteria."

That seemed to do the trick—no subsequent panic or mass hysteria.

We're not comfortable when such things aren't adequately explained.

We need to file it, dismiss it, somewhere deep within our brains.

Because we tend to feel a bit too nervous and quite vulnerable

when the causes of such things are not immediately discernible.

Any explanation—no matter how unlikely—is better than admitting we've got no clue,

and that such a thing could maybe happen to either me or you.

So let me give you a bit of simple, fatherly advice-

A simple rule to live by, one that should pretty much suffice:

Don't push your luck by eating bugs.

You'll be dead quite soon enough!

Smiling in Mozambique
[A Ramble on Unintended Irony]

I'm sitting in the brand, spanking, spiffy, new show room at the local dealership, waiting for my car to be serviced.

There's free coffee, a big, widescreen TV with a weatherman giving us the news on the latest Armageddon; he can't keep himself from smiling.

They also have a full-size playhouse for your kids with a brightly painted mini—car parked next to it like the ones you see at circuses where a half dozen clowns climb out, defying the laws of physics.

Bright, bright, sunlight streaming through windows so spotless, so transparent that you'd walk right through one of them . . . if it weren't for the colorful posters taped to them depicting carefree, happy people driving their shiny new cars . . . their expressions saying: *"You too could be smiling like this!"*

This year's models are displayed around me, like those beach stones that catch your eye and greed . . . but when you take them home . . .

well . . . they never look as good as they did when you first saw them . . . in their sandy showroom.

In front of me, a long glass table trimmed with chrome, magazines fanned out in an enticing display of young, viral men and seductive women in a variety of settings and showrooms . . . smiling . . . of course.

The sports illustrated issue—the one with the latest models of beach babes, their accessories also artfully displayed, proof of the rewards waiting for those . . . who can keep on smiling.

Armani men in Armani suits making more in a day than most can make in a year—the self confident, successful, tanned titans of Olympus . . . always hungry . . . always smiling.

The Wall Street Journal Magazine . . . I'm hopeful . . . perhaps . . . just maybe . . . but no . . . it's just another flashy show room full of smiling models.

Beautiful people have a lot to smile about, so many shiny young ones looking back at you as they drive away, so stylish on a scooter, leaving you in their exhaust, off to some rendezvous of lust and luxury . . .

while you make your way to your cubicle with your cooling coffee and a list of cold calls in your hand.

I had a scooter once myself . . . a Vespa to be exact . . . when I was 16. My mother made me swear I'd always wear a helmet.

Imagine pulling into a packed parking lot of James Dean wannabees leaning on their muscle cars . . . and you're wearing a helmet . . . on a scooter.

That ad had no pleasing resonance for me.

And then I turn the page . . . And there she is . . . a brown young woman in her colorful native garb standing on a beach in Mozambique, the destination of the month for tired executives who need a break from wheeling and dealing the wealth of nations and the manufactured fantasies of mass fulfillment.

But she too is smiling . . . balancing a pile of rotting driftwood precariously perched on her turbaned head, her destination—a slum shanty of storm debris and wreckage she's assembled for a shelter.

How can she be smiling on a beach in Mozambique—with that drunk of a husband and three hungry, stunted kids—looking in a camera that costs more than she will ever earn?

But she knows that she'll be paid much more . . . if she's smiling . . .

if she assumes the appropriate pose of the picturesque.

I wonder if there's a hammer of hot anger beating somewhere deep within her heart . . .

while I'm waiting in this showroom, surrounded by an opulence paid too often by the practiced smiles of others.

Like unintended consequences, unintended irony can be equally disconcerting.

Pass the Advil
[A Rant on the Price of Joy]

Years ago, I remember a very popular book, one that was secretly perused by many but bought by few: *"The Joys of Sex"*

It was pretty imaginative, requiring a significant amount of erotic imagination and side show flexibility.

It would have given that ancient Hindu "tour de force"—*"The Kama Sutra"*-a hot run for the moaning.

I always wondered if anyone had ever written any subsequent extrapolations such as *"The Joys of Diapers"* or *"The Joys of Post— Partum Depression."*

No, I'm not going to launch into a church sponsored diatribe on the responsibilities and dangers of sex.

I'll leave that to the Sunday Shamans who rail against the pitfalls of demon lust while sneaking furtive glances at boyish backsides.

No, this is not meant to be morally instructive.

Aside from *"do unto others . . ."* and *"cause no pain"*, I'm pretty open to most erotic, consensual configurations: if sadist and masochists want to get it on, no problem, as long as their whips and chains and screaming don't keep me awake.

But it does seem to me that we have evolved a necessary amnesia of the price we often have to pay in the pursuit of most of our "joys".

Good thing . . . or no one would ever take any chances and nothing would ever get done.

Ask Leonardo, the Wright Brothers, the gynecologist who designed the Edsel *[Goggle it]*, and writers, especially guys like me who write stuff like this.

Everyone's a critic. I'm sure you've already made a judgment.

But one thing I do know: most 'joys" can give you one hell of a headache!

Now pass the Advil!

Your turn!